TH
O
Q

THE
OSCAR WILDE
QUOTATION BOOK

Compiled by Andrew Russell

SOMERVILLE PRESS

Somerville Press Ltd,
Dromore, Bantry, Co. Cork, Ireland

©Andrew Russell 2023

Designed by Jane Stark
Typeset in Minion Pro
seamistgraphics@gmail.com

ISBN: 978 1 8382544 76

Printed and bound in the EU

FRONT COVER PHOTO:
Oscar Wilde by Napoleon Sarony, c.1882
(Public Domain)

I HAVE NOTHING
TO DECLARE
BUT MY GENIUS.

THE DIFFERENCE
BETWEEN LITERATURE
AND JOURNALISM
IS THAT
JOURNALISM IS
UNREADABLE AND
LITERATURE IS NOT READ.

ONLY
THE SHALLOW
KNOW
THEMSELVES.

WHENEVER
PEOPLE AGREE
WITH ME
I FEEL
I MUST BE WRONG.

THERE ARE ONLY
TWO TYPES OF PEOPLE
WHO ARE REALLY FASCINATING:
PEOPLE WHO KNOW
ABSOLUTELY EVERYTHING
AND PEOPLE WHO KNOW
ABSOLUTELY NOTHING.

You can never be over dressed or over educated.

ANYONE CAN SYMPATHISE

WITH THE SUFFERINGS

OF A FRIEND,

BUT IT REQUIRES

A VERY FINE NATURE

TO SYMPATHISE WITH A

FRIEND'S SUCCESS.

A BORE IS SOMEONE
WHO DEPRIVES YOU
OF SOLITUDE
WITHOUT
PROVIDING YOU
WITH COMPANY.

LIFE IS
TOO IMPORTANT
A THING
EVER TO
TALK SERIOUSLY
ABOUT.

BETWEEN MEN
AND WOMEN
THERE IS
NO FRIENDSHIP POSSIBLE.
THERE IS PASSION,
ENMITY AND LOVE
BUT NO FRIENDSHIP.

THE
SUPREME
VICE
IS
SHALLOWNESS.

EDUCATION IS

AN ADMIRABLE THING,

BUT IT IS WELL TO REMEMBER

FROM TIME TO TIME

THAT NOTHING THAT IS

WORTH KNOWING

CAN BE TAUGHT.

SOME

CAUSE HAPPINESS

WHEREVER THEY GO;

OTHERS

WHENEVER THEY GO.

IF YOU ARE

NOT TOO LONG,

I WILL WAIT FOR YOU

ALL MY LIFE.

AN OPTIMIST

WILL TELL YOU

THE GLASS IS HALF FULL:

THE PESSIMIST,

HALF EMPTY;

AND THE ENGINEER

WILL TELL YOU

THE GLASS IS

TWICE THE SIZE IT NEEDS TO BE.

IT'S BEAUTY
THAT CAPTURES
YOUR ATTENTION,
PERSONALITY
THAT CAPTURES
YOUR HEART.

SOCIETY EXISTS
ONLY AS A
MENTAL CONCEPT;
IN THE REAL WORLD
THERE ARE
ONLY INDIVIDUALS.

BIGAMY

IS HAVING

ONE WIFE TOO MANY.

MONOGAMY

IS THE SAME.

LIFE IS NEVER FAIR,

AND PERHAPS

IT IS A GOOD THING

FOR MOST OF US

THAT IT IS NOT.

IT IS ABSURD
TO DIVIDE PEOPLE
INTO GOOD OR BAD.
PEOPLE ARE EITHER
CHARMING
OR TEDIOUS.

WORK
IS THE
CURSE
OF THE
DRINKING
CLASSES.

THERE IS
ONLY ONE
THING IN LIFE
WORSE THAN
BEING TALKED ABOUT
AND THAT IS
NOT BEING TALKED ABOUT.

WHEN I WAS YOUNG
I THOUGHT THAT
MONEY WAS
THE MOST IMPORTANT
THING IN LIFE;
NOW THAT I AM OLD
I KNOW IT IS.

THE OLD
BELIEVE EVERYTHING,
THE MIDDLE-AGED
SUSPECT EVERYTHING,
THE YOUNG
KNOW EVERYTHING.

LAUGHTER
IS NOT AT ALL
A BAD BEGINNING
FOR A FRIENDSHIP,
AND IT IS
FAR THE BEST
ENDING FOR ONE.

MARRIAGE
IS A
LONG DULL MEAL
WITH
DESSERT SERVED
AT THE BEGINNING.

LIFE
IMITATES ART
FAR MORE
THAN
ART
IMITATES LIFE.

BY GIVING US
THE OPINIONS
OF THE UNEDUCATED,
JOURNALISM
KEEPS US IN TOUCH
WITH THE IGNORANCE
OF THE COMMUNITY.

WOMEN
ARE MADE
TO BE LOVED,
NOT UNDERSTOOD.

TO LIVE IS
THE RAREST THING
IN THE WORLD.
MOST PEOPLE EXIST,
THAT IS ALL.

FASHION IS
A FORM
OF UGLINESS
SO INTOLERABLE
THAT WE HAVE TO
ALTER IT
EVERY SIX MONTHS.

WE ARE EACH
OUR OWN DEVIL
AND WE MAKE
THIS WORLD
OUR HELL.

WE HAVE
REALLY EVERYTHING
IN COMMON
WITH AMERICA
NOWADAYS
EXCEPT, OF COURSE,
LANGUAGE.

I AM
SO CLEVER
THAT
SOMETIMES
I DON'T
UNDERSTAND
A SINGLE WORD
I AM SAYING.

THE LIFE

OF A MAN

IS NO MORE THAN

THE LIFE

OF A FLOWER.

ALL WOMEN
BECOME LIKE
THEIR MOTHERS.
THAT IS
THEIR TRAGEDY.
NO MAN DOES.
THAT'S HIS.

Religion

is like

a blind man

looking in

a black room

for a black cat

and finding it.

THE ENGLISH
COUNTRY GENTLEMAN
GALLOPING
AFTER A FOX:
THE UNSPEAKABLE
IN PURSUIT OF
THE UNEATABLE.

I CAN NEVER
TRAVEL WITHOUT
MY DIARY:
ONE SHOULD ALWAYS
HAVE SOMETHING
SENSATIONAL TO READ
ON THE TRAIN.

ONE SHOULD NEVER
TRUST A WOMAN
WHO TELLS YOU
HER REAL AGE.
A WOMAN WHO
WOULD TELL ONE THAT
WOULD TELL ONE
EVERYTHING.

ART

IS THE MOST
INTENSE
INDIVIDUALISM
THAT THE WORLD
HAS EVER KNOWN.

I THINK THAT
GOD,
IN CREATING MAN,
OVERESTIMATED
HIS ABILITY.

MURDER

IS ALWAYS

A MISTAKE.

ONE SHOULD NEVER

DO ANYTHING THAT

ONE CANNOT TALK

ABOUT AFTER DINNER.

A CIGARETTE

IS THE PERFECT

TYPE OF PLEASURE.

IT IS EXQUISITE

AND LEAVES ONE

UNSATISFIED.

KEEP LOVE
IN YOUR HEART.
A LIFE WITHOUT IT
IS LIKE
A SUNLESS GARDEN
WHEN THE
FLOWERS ARE DEAD.

A GENTLEMAN

IS ONE

WHO NEVER HURTS

ANYONE'S FEELINGS

UNINTENTIONALLY.

MORALITY
IS THE ATTITUDE
WE ADOPT
TOWARDS PEOPLE
WE PERSONALLY
DISLIKE.

In my youth
I would do anything
in the world,
except
take exercise,
get up early
or be respectable.

THE TRUTH IS
RARELY PURE
AND NEVER SIMPLE.

●

NO MAN IS
RICH ENOUGH
TO BUY BACK
HIS PAST.

WHEN YOU
REALLY WANT LOVE,
YOU WILL FIND IT
WAITING FOR YOU.

I HAVE
SIMPLE TASTES.
I AM ALWAYS
SATISFIED
WITH THE BEST.

WHEN THE GODS
WISH TO
PUNISH US
THEY ANSWER
OUR PRAYERS.

RIDICULE
IS THE TRIBUTE
PAID TO
THE GENIUS
BY THE
MEDIOCRITIES.

SUCCESS

IS A SCIENCE;

IF YOU HAVE

THE CONDITIONS,

YOU GET

THE RESULT.

A MAN
CAN BE HAPPY
WITH ANY WOMAN
AS LONG AS
HE DOES NOT
LOVE HER.

WE ARE ALL
IN THE GUTTER,
BUT SOME OF US
ARE LOOKING
AT THE STARS.

A MAN'S FACE
IS HIS
AUTOBIOGRAPHY.
A WOMAN'S FACE
IS HER
WORK OF FICTION.

TO EXPECT
THE UNEXPECTED
SHOWS A
THOROUGHLY
MODERN
INTELLECT.

THE ANSWERS

ARE ALL

OUT THERE,

WE JUST NEED

TO ASK

THE RIGHT QUESTIONS.

ALWAYS FORGIVE

YOUR ENEMIES;

NOTHING ANNOYS

THEM MORE.

THE MYSTERY
OF LOVE
IS GREATER THAN
THE MYSTERY
OF DEATH.

IT TAKES

A GREAT DEAL

OF COURAGE

TO SEE THE WORLD

IN ALL ITS

TAINTED GLORY

AND STILL

TO LOVE IT.

THERE IS NO SIN EXCEPT STUPIDITY.

WE LIVE
IN AN AGE
WHEN
UNNECESSARY THINGS
ARE OUR
ONLY NECESSITIES.

I DON'T WANT
TO GO TO
HEAVEN.
NONE OF MY FRIENDS
ARE THERE.

ANYONE

WHO LIVES

WITHIN THEIR MEANS

SUFFERS FROM

A LACK OF

IMAGINATION.

MY OWN BUSINESS

BORES ME

TO DEATH;

I PREFER

OTHER PEOPLE'S.

A CYNIC

IS A MAN

WHO KNOWS THE PRICE

OF EVERYTHING

BUT THE VALUE

OF NOTHING.

IT'S NOT
WHETHER
YOU WIN
OR LOSE,
IT'S HOW YOU
PLACE THE BLAME.

IT IS ONLY

THE MODERN

THAT EVER BECOMES

OLD-FASHIONED.

THE BEST WAY TO

ENJOY YOUR JOB

IS TO

IMAGINE YOURSELF

WITHOUT ONE.

TO LOVE ONESELF

IS THE

BEGINNING

OF A

LIFELONG ROMANCE.

BEHIND EVERY
EXQUISITE THING
THAT EXISTED,
THERE WAS ALWAYS
SOMETHING
TRAGIC.

A MAN WHO
DOES NOT
THINK FOR HIMSELF
DOES NOT THINK
AT ALL.

A PESSIMIST
IS ONE WHO,
WHEN HE HAS
A CHOICE
OF TWO EVILS,
CHOOSES BOTH.

MODERATION

IS A FATAL THING.

NOTHING

SUCCEEDS

LIKE EXCESS.

A PASSION
FOR PLEASURE
IS THE SECRET OF
REMAINING
YOUNG.

THE ONLY WAY
TO GET RID OF
TEMPTATION
IS TO YIELD
TO IT.

EVERYTHING IN MODERATION, INCLUDING MODERATION.

EXPERIENCE
IS SIMPLY
THE NAME
WE GIVE
OUR MISTAKES.

THE NICEST THING
IN THE WORLD
IS TO DO
A GOOD DEED
ANONYMOUSLY
AND HAVE
SOMEONE FIND OUT.

TRUE FRIENDS
STAB YOU
IN THE FRONT.

He hasn't a single
redeeming vice.

•

All great ideas
are dangerous.

FRIENDSHIP

IS FAR MORE

TRAGIC

THAN LOVE:

IT LASTS LONGER.

BE YOURSELF; EVERYONE ELSE IS ALREADY TAKEN.

THE WORLD
IS A STAGE,
BUT THE PLAY
IS BADLY CAST.

AMBITION

IS THE

LAST REFUGE

OF THE

FAILURE.

No
GOOD DEED
GOES
UNPUNISHED.

THE
SECRET
OF LIFE
IS SUFFERING.

I CAN RESIST ANYTHING EXCEPT TEMPTATION.